If Lost, Please Return To:

_____

Dedication

This Bible Study Journal is dedicated to all the people out there who want to record their study of the Bible and document their findings in the process.

You are my inspiration for producing books and I'm honored to be a part of keeping all of your Bible Study notes and records organized. This journal notebook will help you record the details of studying the Bible.

Thoughtfully put together with these sections to record: Weekly Goals, Scripture Notes, Praise & Prayer, SOAP, & Reflection.

How to Use this Book

The purpose of this book is to keep all of your Bible Study notes all in one place. It will help keep you organized.

This Bible Study Journal will allow you to accurately document every detail about your Bible Study adventures.

Here are examples of the prompts for you to fill in and write about your experience in this book:

1. Weekly Goals - Each week there's a place for journaling your personal, life goals.

2. Scripture Notes - Blank lined space to record your scripture verse and notes.

3. Praise & Prayer - Write your praises and prayer requests.

4. SOAP - Scripture, Observation, Application, and Prayer.

5. Reflection - Includes question prompts about your study.

Monday

Today's Goals

Tuesday

Today's Goals

Wednesday

Today's Goals

Thursday

Today's Goals

Friday

Today's Goals

Saturday

Today's Goals

Sunday

Today's Goals

Notes

Bible Study

Date:

Today's Study

Scripture

Praise

Prayer

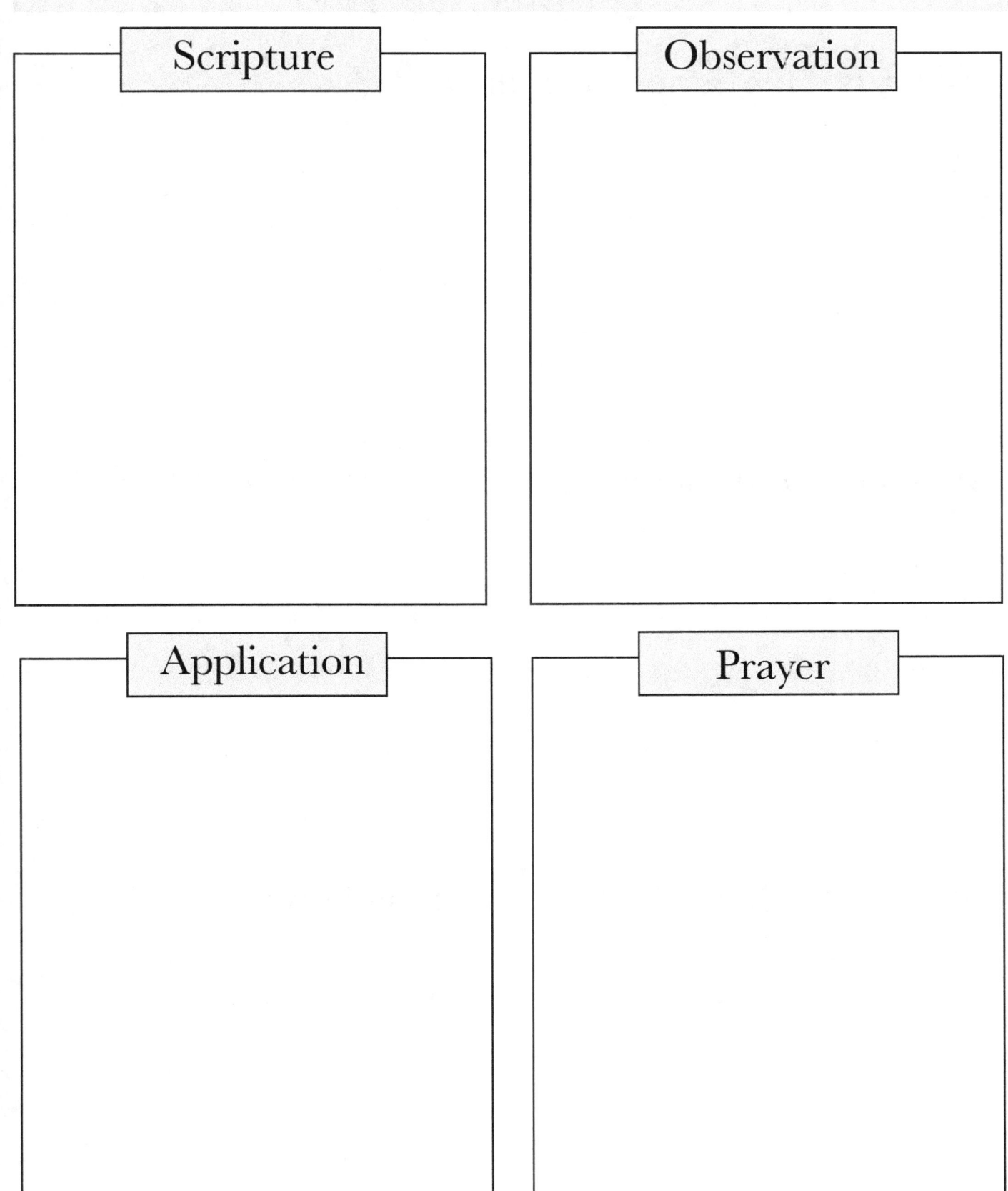

Reflection

What Is This Scripture Telling Me?

_____
_____
_____
_____

Why Did God Include This Scripture In The Bible?

_____
_____
_____
_____

What Do I Need To Further Study From This Verse?

_____
_____
_____
_____

Bible Study

Date:

Today's Study

Scripture

Praise

Prayer

S.O.A.P.

Scripture

Observation

Application

Prayer

Reflection

What Is This Scripture Telling Me?

_____
_____
_____
_____
_____

Why Did God Include This Scripture In The Bible?

_____
_____
_____
_____
_____

What Do I Need To Further Study From This Verse?

_____
_____
_____
_____
_____

Bible Study

Date:

Today's Study

Scripture

Praise

Prayer

S.O.A.P.

Scripture

Observation

Application

Prayer

Reflection

What Is This Scripture Telling Me?

_____
_____
_____
_____

Why Did God Include This Scripture In The Bible?

_____
_____
_____
_____

What Do I Need To Further Study From This Verse?

_____
_____
_____
_____

Bible Study

Date:

Today's Study

Scripture

Praise

Prayer

S.O.A.P.

Scripture

Observation

Application

Prayer

Reflection

What Is This Scripture Telling Me?

Why Did God Include This Scripture In The Bible?

What Do I Need To Further Study From This Verse?

Bible Study

Date:

Today's Study

Scripture

Praise

Prayer

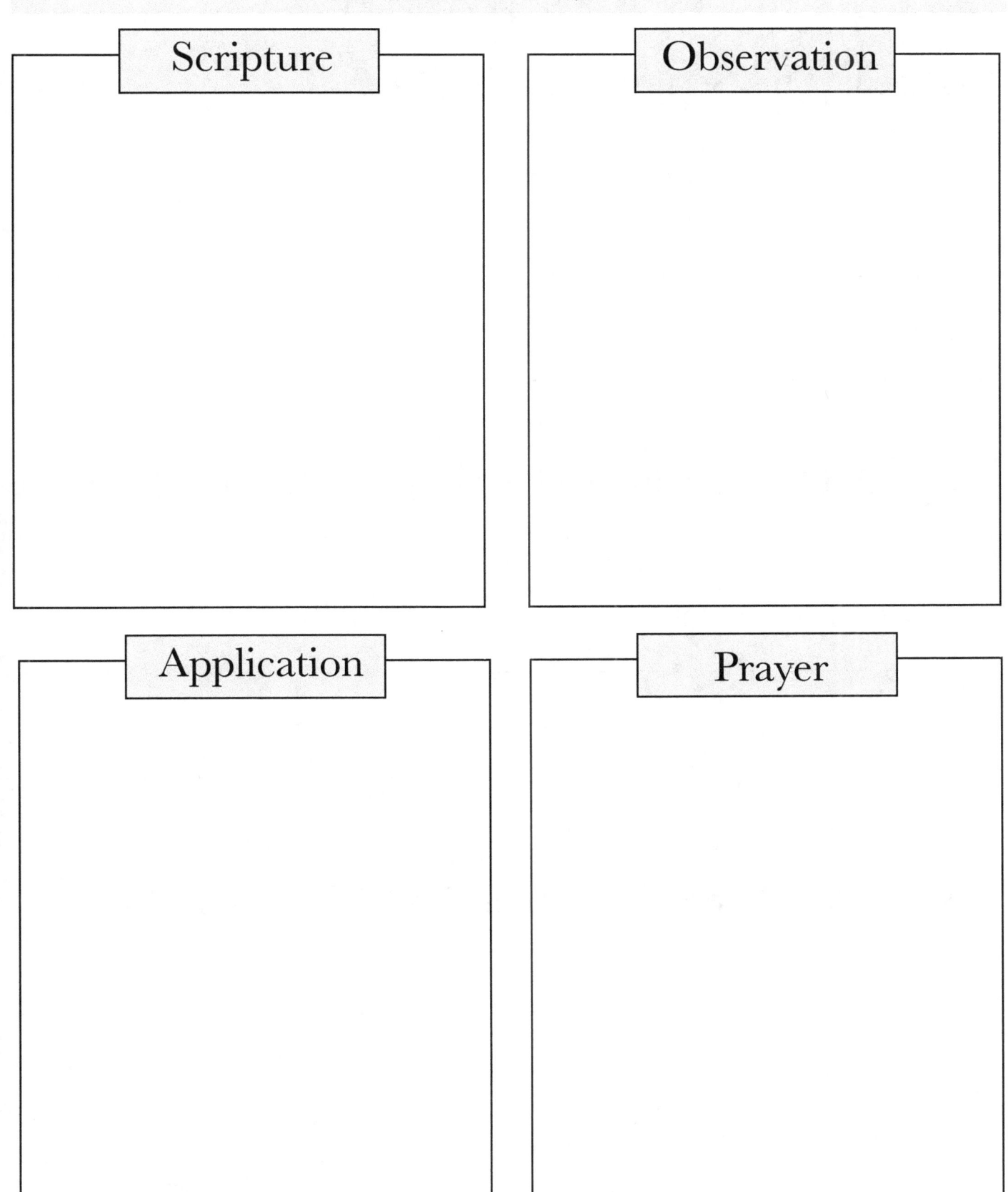

Reflection

What Is This Scripture Telling Me?

Why Did God Include This Scripture In The Bible?

What Do I Need To Further Study From This Verse?

Bible Study

Date:

Today's Study

Scripture

Praise

Prayer

S.O.A.P.

Scripture

Observation

Application

Prayer

Reflection

What Is This Scripture Telling Me?

_____
_____
_____
_____

Why Did God Include This Scripture In The Bible?

_____
_____
_____
_____
_____

What Do I Need To Further Study From This Verse?

_____
_____
_____
_____

Bible Study

Date:

Today's Study

Scripture

Praise

Prayer

S.O.A.P.

Scripture

Observation

Application

Prayer

Reflection

What Is This Scripture Telling Me?

Why Did God Include This Scripture In The Bible?

What Do I Need To Further Study From This Verse?

Monday

Today's Goals

Tuesday

Today's Goals

Wednesday

Today's Goals

Thursday

Today's Goals

Friday

Today's Goals

Saturday

Today's Goals

Sunday

Today's Goals

Notes

Bible Study

Date:

Today's Study

Scripture

Praise

Prayer

S.O.A.P.

Scripture

Observation

Application

Prayer

Reflection

What Is This Scripture Telling Me?

_____
_____
_____
_____
_____

Why Did God Include This Scripture In The Bible?

_____
_____
_____
_____
_____

What Do I Need To Further Study From This Verse?

_____
_____
_____
_____
_____

Bible Study

Date:

Today's Study

Scripture

Praise

Prayer

S.O.A.P.

Scripture

Observation

Application

Prayer

Reflection

What Is This Scripture Telling Me?

Why Did God Include This Scripture In The Bible?

What Do I Need To Further Study From This Verse?

Bible Study

Date:

Today's Study

Scripture

Praise

Prayer

S.O.A.P.

Scripture

Observation

Application

Prayer

Reflection

What Is This Scripture Telling Me?

_____
_____
_____
_____
_____

Why Did God Include This Scripture In The Bible?

_____
_____
_____
_____
_____

What Do I Need To Further Study From This Verse?

_____
_____
_____
_____

Bible Study

Date:

Today's Study

Scripture

Praise

Prayer

S.O.A.P.

Scripture

Observation

Application

Prayer

Reflection

What Is This Scripture Telling Me?

Why Did God Include This Scripture In The Bible?

What Do I Need To Further Study From This Verse?

Bible Study

Date:

Today's Study

Scripture

Praise

Prayer

S.O.A.P.

Scripture

Observation

Application

Prayer

Reflection

What Is This Scripture Telling Me?

Why Did God Include This Scripture In The Bible?

What Do I Need To Further Study From This Verse?

Bible Study

Date:

Today's Study

Scripture

Praise

Prayer

S.O.A.P.

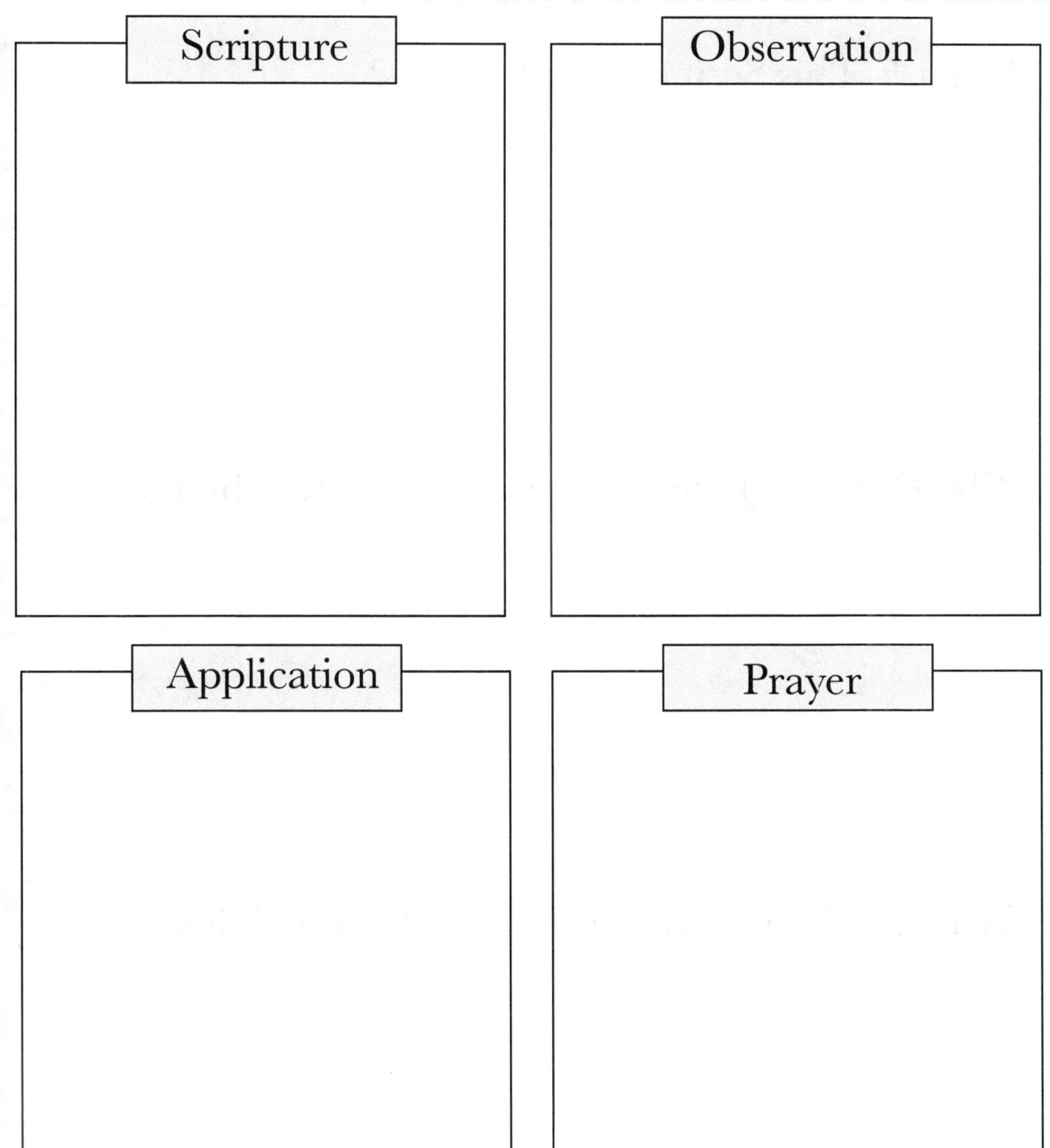

Reflection

What Is This Scripture Telling Me?

_____
_____
_____
_____

Why Did God Include This Scripture In The Bible?

_____
_____
_____
_____

What Do I Need To Further Study From This Verse?

_____
_____
_____
_____

Bible Study

Date:

Today's Study

Scripture

Praise

Prayer

S.O.A.P.

Scripture

Observation

Application

Prayer

Reflection

What Is This Scripture Telling Me?

_____
_____
_____
_____

Why Did God Include This Scripture In The Bible?

_____
_____
_____
_____

What Do I Need To Further Study From This Verse?

_____
_____
_____
_____

Monday

Today's Goals

Tuesday

Today's Goals

Wednesday

Today's Goals

Thursday

Today's Goals

Friday

Today's Goals

Saturday

Today's Goals

Sunday

Today's Goals

Notes

Bible Study

Date:

Today's Study

Scripture

Praise

Prayer

S.O.A.P.

Scripture

Observation

Application

Prayer

Reflection

What Is This Scripture Telling Me?

Why Did God Include This Scripture In The Bible?

What Do I Need To Further Study From This Verse?

Bible Study

Date:

Today's Study

Scripture

Praise

Prayer

S.O.A.P.

Scripture

Observation

Application

Prayer

Reflection

What Is This Scripture Telling Me?

_____
_____
_____
_____

Why Did God Include This Scripture In The Bible?

_____
_____
_____
_____

What Do I Need To Further Study From This Verse?

_____
_____
_____
_____

Bible Study

Date:

Today's Study

Scripture

Praise

Prayer

S.O.A.P.

Scripture

Observation

Application

Prayer

Reflection

What Is This Scripture Telling Me?

_____
_____
_____
_____

Why Did God Include This Scripture In The Bible?

_____
_____
_____
_____

What Do I Need To Further Study From This Verse?

_____
_____
_____
_____

Bible Study

Date:

Today's Study

Scripture

Praise

Prayer

S.O.A.P.

Scripture

Observation

Application

Prayer

Reflection

What Is This Scripture Telling Me?

_____
_____
_____
_____

Why Did God Include This Scripture In The Bible?

_____
_____
_____
_____

What Do I Need To Further Study From This Verse?

_____
_____
_____
_____

Bible Study

Date:

Today's Study

Scripture

Praise

Prayer

S.O.A.P.

Scripture

Observation

Application

Prayer

Reflection

What Is This Scripture Telling Me?

_____
_____
_____
_____

Why Did God Include This Scripture In The Bible?

_____
_____
_____
_____

What Do I Need To Further Study From This Verse?

_____
_____
_____
_____

Bible Study

Date:

Today's Study

Scripture

Praise

Prayer

S.O.A.P.

Scripture

Observation

Application

Prayer

Reflection

What Is This Scripture Telling Me?

_____
_____
_____
_____

Why Did God Include This Scripture In The Bible?

_____
_____
_____
_____

What Do I Need To Further Study From This Verse?

_____
_____
_____
_____

Bible Study

Date:

Today's Study

Scripture

Praise

Prayer

S.O.A.P.

Scripture

Observation

Application

Prayer

Reflection

What Is This Scripture Telling Me?

Why Did God Include This Scripture In The Bible?

What Do I Need To Further Study From This Verse?

Monday

Today's Goals

_____
_____
_____
_____

Tuesday

Today's Goals

_____
_____
_____
_____
_____

Wednesday

Today's Goals

_____
_____
_____
_____
_____

Thursday

Today's Goals

_____
_____
_____
_____

Friday

Today's Goals

Saturday

Today's Goals

Sunday

Today's Goals

Notes

Bible Study

Date:

Today's Study

Scripture

Praise

Prayer

S.O.A.P.

Scripture

Observation

Application

Prayer

Reflection

What Is This Scripture Telling Me?

Why Did God Include This Scripture In The Bible?

What Do I Need To Further Study From This Verse?

Bible Study

Date:

Today's Study

Scripture

Praise

Prayer

S.O.A.P.

Scripture

Observation

Application

Prayer

Reflection

What Is This Scripture Telling Me?

_____
_____
_____
_____

Why Did God Include This Scripture In The Bible?

_____
_____
_____
_____

What Do I Need To Further Study From This Verse?

_____
_____
_____
_____

Bible Study

Date:

Today's Study

Scripture

Praise

Prayer

S.O.A.P.

Scripture

Observation

Application

Prayer

Reflection

What Is This Scripture Telling Me?

Why Did God Include This Scripture In The Bible?

What Do I Need To Further Study From This Verse?

Bible Study

Date:

Today's Study

Scripture

Praise

Prayer

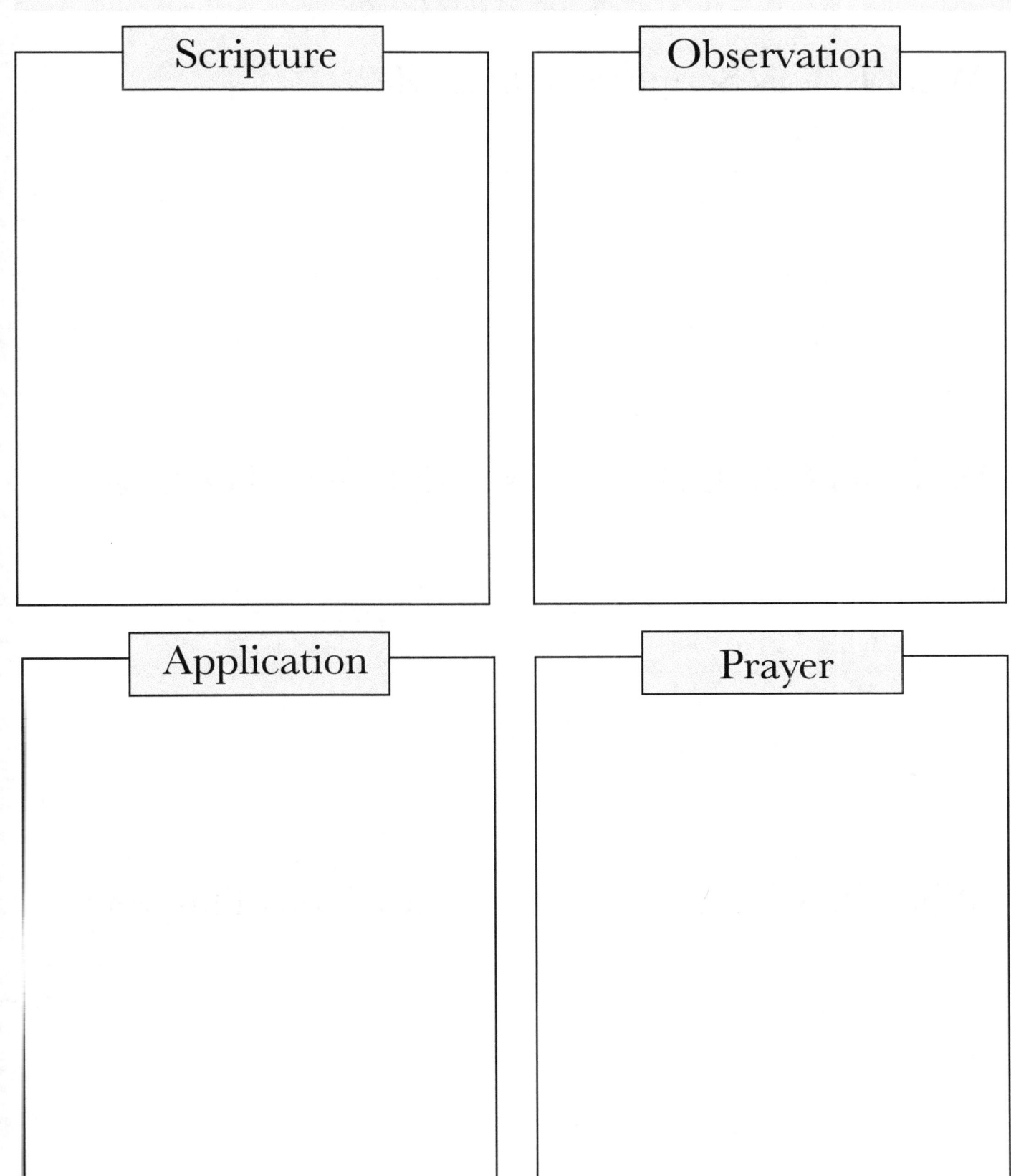

Reflection

What Is This Scripture Telling Me?

Why Did God Include This Scripture In The Bible?

What Do I Need To Further Study From This Verse?

Bible Study

Date:

Today's Study

Scripture

Praise

Prayer

S.O.A.P.

Scripture

Observation

Application

Prayer

Reflection

What Is This Scripture Telling Me?

_____
_____
_____
_____

Why Did God Include This Scripture In The Bible?

_____
_____
_____
_____

What Do I Need To Further Study From This Verse?

_____
_____
_____
_____

Bible Study

Date:

Today's Study

Scripture

Praise

Prayer

S.O.A.P.

Scripture

Observation

Application

Prayer

Reflection

What Is This Scripture Telling Me?

___

Why Did God Include This Scripture In The Bible?

___

What Do I Need To Further Study From This Verse?

___

Bible Study

Date:

Today's Study

Scripture

Praise

Prayer

S.O.A.P.

Scripture

Observation

Application

Prayer

Reflection

What Is This Scripture Telling Me?

_____
_____
_____
_____
_____

Why Did God Include This Scripture In The Bible?

_____
_____
_____
_____
_____

What Do I Need To Further Study From This Verse?

_____
_____
_____
_____
_____

Monday

Today's Goals

Tuesday

Today's Goals

Wednesday

Today's Goals

Thursday

Today's Goals

Friday

Today's Goals

Saturday

Today's Goals

Sunday

Today's Goals

Notes

Bible Study

Date:

Today's Study

Scripture

Praise

Prayer

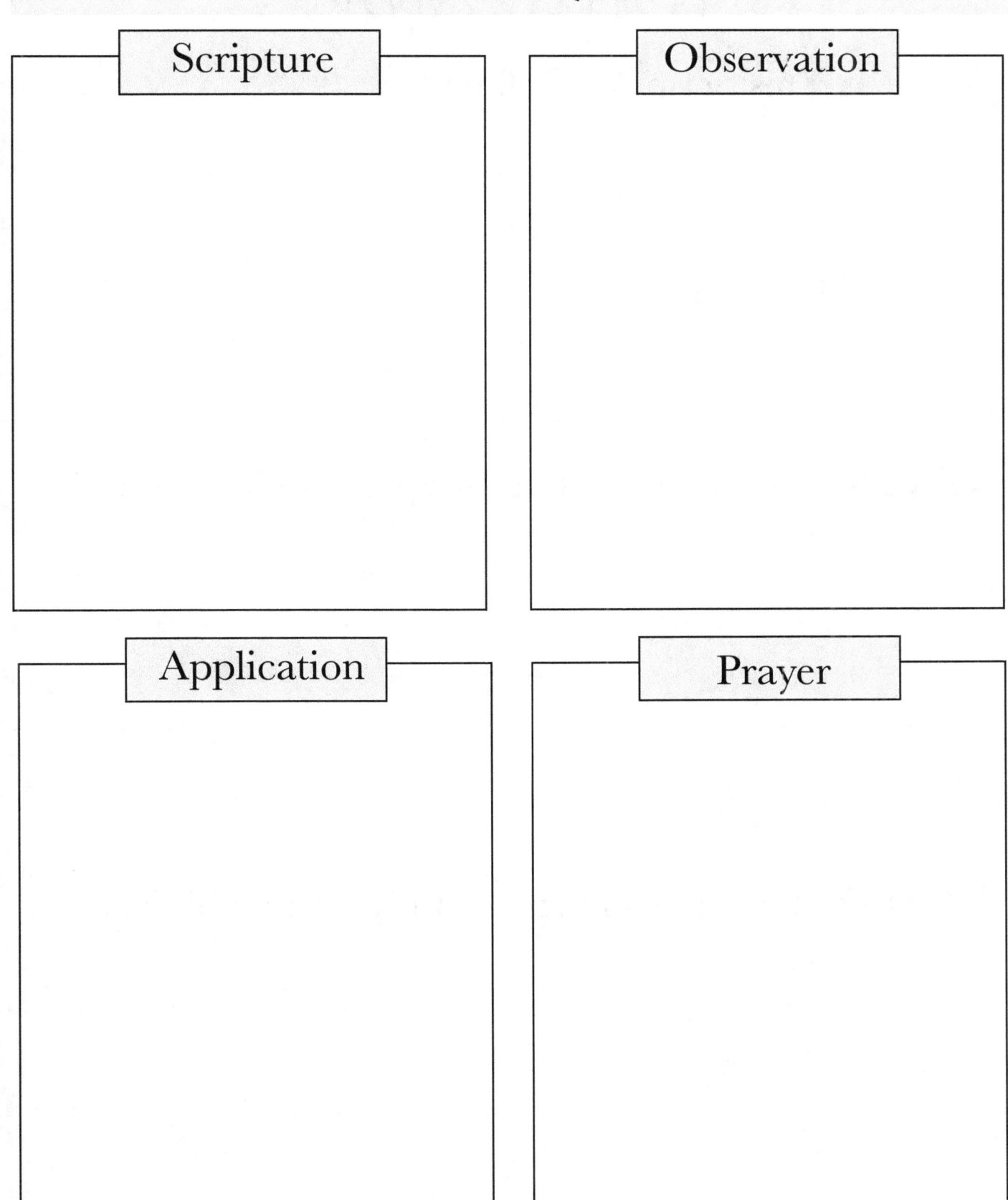

Reflection

What Is This Scripture Telling Me?

Why Did God Include This Scripture In The Bible?

What Do I Need To Further Study From This Verse?

Bible Study

Date:

Today's Study

Scripture

Praise

Prayer

S.O.A.P.

Scripture	Observation
Application	Prayer

Reflection

What Is This Scripture Telling Me?

Why Did God Include This Scripture In The Bible?

What Do I Need To Further Study From This Verse?

Bible Study

Date:

Today's Study

Scripture

Praise

Prayer

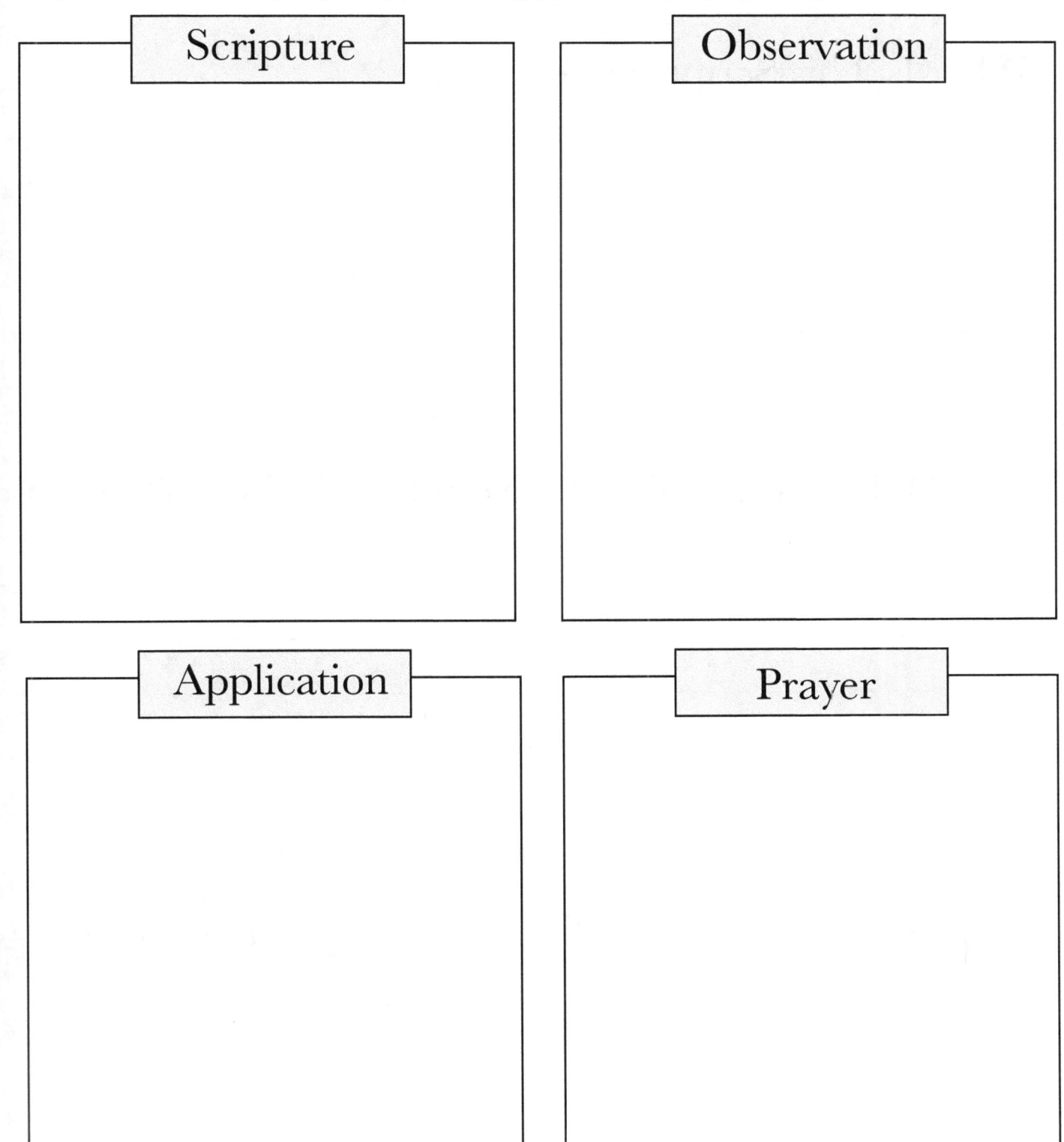

Reflection

What Is This Scripture Telling Me?

Why Did God Include This Scripture In The Bible?

What Do I Need To Further Study From This Verse?

Bible Study

Date:

Today's Study

Scripture

Praise

Prayer

S.O.A.P.

Scripture

Observation

Application

Prayer

Reflection

What Is This Scripture Telling Me?

_____
_____
_____
_____
_____

Why Did God Include This Scripture In The Bible?

_____
_____
_____
_____
_____

What Do I Need To Further Study From This Verse?

_____
_____
_____
_____
_____

Bible Study

Date:

Today's Study

Scripture

Praise

Prayer

S.O.A.P.

Scripture

Observation

Application

Prayer

Reflection

What Is This Scripture Telling Me?

Why Did God Include This Scripture In The Bible?

What Do I Need To Further Study From This Verse?

Bible Study

Date:

Today's Study

Scripture

Praise

Prayer

S.O.A.P.

Scripture

Observation

Application

Prayer

Reflection

What Is This Scripture Telling Me?

_____
_____
_____
_____

Why Did God Include This Scripture In The Bible?

_____
_____
_____
_____

What Do I Need To Further Study From This Verse?

_____
_____
_____
_____

Bible Study

Date:

Today's Study

Scripture

Praise

Prayer

S.O.A.P.

Scripture

Observation

Application

Prayer

Reflection

What Is This Scripture Telling Me?

Why Did God Include This Scripture In The Bible?

What Do I Need To Further Study From This Verse?